The Life Cycle of a

Butterfly

Bobbie Kalman
Illustrated by Margaret Amy Reiach
Crabtree Publishing Company

www.crabtreebooks.com

The Life Cycle Series
A Bobbie Kalman Book

For my daughter Samantha, a beautiful butterfly

Dedicated by Maggie Reiach
For Sommer, a vision of nature's strength and beauty

Author and Editor-in-Chief
Bobbie Kalman

Editors
Kathryn Smithyman
Amanda Bishop
Niki Walker

Cover design
Campbell Creative Services

Computer design
Margaret Amy Reiach

Production coordinator
Heather Fitzpatrick

Photo researcher
Heather Fitzpatrick

Consultant
Patricia Loesche, Ph.D., Animal Behavior Program,
Department of Psychology, University of Washington

Photographs
Frank S. Balthis: pages 16 (bottom), 24, 26 (top), 27, 31
John Daly: pages 16 (top), 17, 18, 19, 20, 21, 22 (bottom),
 23 (top)
Robert McCaw: pages 22 (top), 23 (bottom), 26 (bottom)
Tom Stack and Associates: Jeff Foott: 25
Other images by Adobe Image Library, Digital Stock
and Digital Vision

Illustrations
All illustrations by Margaret Amy Reiach, except the following:
Antoinette "Cookie" DeBiasi: page 7 (top)
Tiffany Wybouw: pages 15 (top), 17, 30 (bottom center),
 31 (top left and right)

Crabtree Publishing Company
www.crabtreebooks.com   1-800-387-7650

PMB 16A	612 Welland Avenue	73 Lime Walk
350 Fifth Avenue	St. Catharines	Headington
Suite 3308	Ontario	Oxford
New York, NY	Canada	OX3 7AD
10118	L2M 5V6	United Kingdom

Cataloging in Publication Data
Kalman, Bobbie
   The life cycle of a butterfly / Bobbie Kalman;
illustrated by Margaret Amy Reiach.
       p. cm. -- (The life cycle)
       Includes index.
   Describes the various stages of a monarch butterfly's life, from egg
to pupa to caterpillar to butterfly, as well as its migration and the
dangers it faces.
   ISBN 0-7787-0650-8 (RLB) -- ISBN 0-7787-0680-X (pbk.)
   1. Butterflies--Life cycles--Juvenile literature. [1. Monarch butterfly.
2. Butterflies. 3. Caterpillars.] I. Reiach, Margaret Amy, ill. II. Title.
   QL544.2 .K352 2002
   595.78′9--dc21
                                                  2001037212

Contents

tailed jay

banded orange

rice paper

zebra longwing

Beautiful butterflies

These butterflies are beautiful, but they did not always look as they do now. Just a few weeks ago, they were not butterflies at all! They were caterpillars and looked like worms with stubby legs. Their bodies changed many times before they became adult butterflies. Read on to learn more about these changes.

white peacock

tiger longwing

Grecian shoemaker

gulf fritillary

cattleheart

queen

owl

monarch

Julia

red lacewing

small postman

great eggfly

plain tiger

sulphur

How many of
these butterflies
have you seen?

giant swallowtail

5

What is a butterfly?

A butterfly is an **insect**. Insect bodies have three sections—a head, a **thorax**, and an **abdomen**. All insects have six legs and some, including butterflies, have wings. They also have two feelers called **antennae**. Butterflies smell with their feelers and taste with their feet.

*Butterfly wings are covered with millions of tiny **scales**. The scales give wings color and help the insect fly. If you touch a butterfly's wing, the scales will rub off on your fingers and the wing will be damaged.*

A butterfly's body

A butterfly is built for flying and gliding. It has large wings and a tiny lightweight body. Its **compound eyes** see colors and patterns on flowers that our eyes cannot see. The patterns help guide the butterfly to the **nectar** at the center of a flower. A butterfly uses its long tongue, called a **proboscis**, to suck up the nectar.

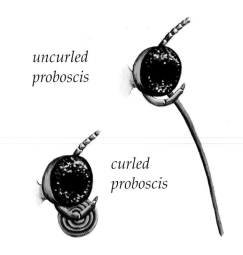

uncurled proboscis

curled proboscis

The proboscis straightens to reach into a flower and curls up when not in use.

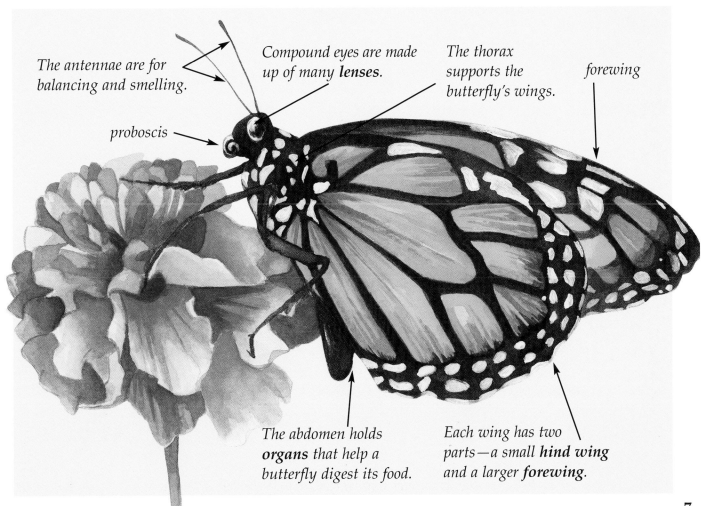

The antennae are for balancing and smelling.

*Compound eyes are made up of many **lenses**.*

The thorax supports the butterfly's wings.

forewing

proboscis

*The abdomen holds **organs** that help a butterfly digest its food.*

*Each wing has two parts—a small **hind wing** and a larger **forewing**.*

7

What is a life cycle?

An animal's **life cycle** is made up of the stages in its life from the time it is born to the time it becomes an adult that can make babies. Each life cycle has the same stages—hatching or being born, growing, and changing into an adult. Life cycles continue as long as there are animals that can make babies.

Here for a short time

An animal's life cycle is not the same as its **life span**. A life span is the length of time an animal is alive. Most butterflies have a short life span. They live for only a few weeks.

Monarchs live longer!

Monarchs live longer than other butterflies do. Their life span depends on when they are born. Monarchs that are born in the spring live four to five weeks, but those born in the fall live for several months.

From egg to butterfly

A butterfly goes through four stages in its life cycle: the egg, **larva**, **pupa**, and adult.

When an adult female lays her eggs, the life cycle begins again.

1 *The first stage of the life cycle is the egg.*

4

The adult butterfly comes out of the case and is ready to fly.

2 *The larva hatches from the egg. It is called a caterpillar.*

*The caterpillar makes a case around itself. The insect is now a **pupa**.*

3 *When the **chrysalis**, or case, looks clear, the pupa has become a butterfly.*

9

The magnificent monarch

This book is about the life cycle of the monarch butterfly. Monarchs are found in more places than other butterflies are. It is easy to spot their orange-and-black wings. Monarchs can fly much farther than other butterflies can. Each year monarchs fly long distances.

Monarchs need milkweed!

Monarchs lay their eggs only on milkweed plants. If there are no milkweed plants in an area, there will be no monarchs either!

Loaded with eggs

When you lift a milkweed leaf, you will likely find one or more tiny monarch eggs stuck to its underside.

This milkweed plant is loaded with monarch eggs, which look like tiny dots. They were laid by more than one butterfly.

Growing inside the egg

At first, the monarch eggs are white, but they soon turn dark gray. A caterpillar is growing inside each egg. It feeds on the **yolk**, which is food stored inside the egg.

Let me out!

After three to six days, the caterpillar is ready to hatch. It chews its way out of the eggshell and then eats it.

*The eggshell is the caterpillar's first meal. It is full of vitamins and minerals. The caterpillar needs these **nutrients** to help it grow.*

11

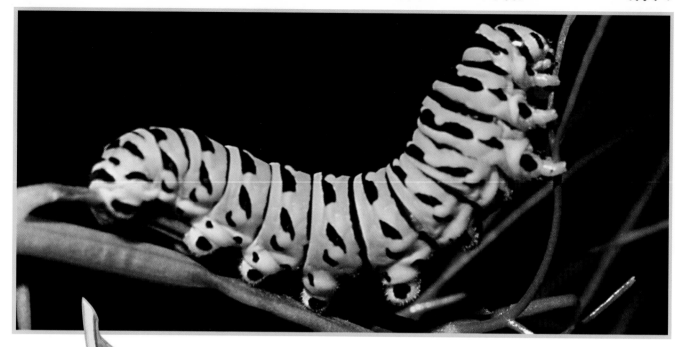

Hungry caterpillars

The tiny caterpillar is green when it hatches. Soon its skin is covered with spots and stripes. Once they appear, the caterpillar gets down to work—eating!

Chomp, chomp, chomp!

The caterpillar has strong jaws for chewing leaves. Milkweed leaves are the only food it eats. The caterpillar eats about 30 leaves to get ready for the next stage of its life cycle. The more it eats, the bigger it gets.

As it eats, the caterpillar gets bigger. It grows so much that it weighs 3000 times as much as it did when it hatched.

Caterpillar parts

A caterpillar has simple eyes that see only light and dark. It finds its way by using its **tentacles**. Each caterpillar has a **spinneret** under its head for making silk. The silk plays a very important part in the next stage of the life cycle.

A closer look

Have you ever seen a caterpillar up close? Look at this one and study its body parts. Now look at the butterfly on page 7 and compare its body parts to those of this caterpillar. Which are the same? Which are different?

The caterpillar feels with its tentacles.

A caterpillar breathes through tiny holes, called **spiracles**, *along its body.*

Its rear tentacles are also for feeling. Some caterpillars do not have any tentacles.

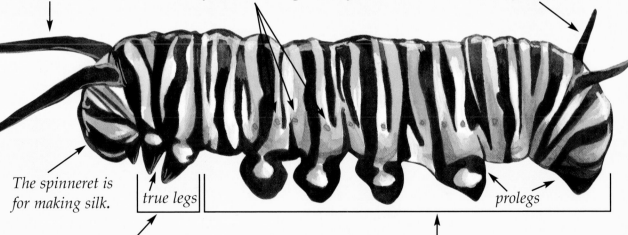

The spinneret is for making silk.

true legs

prolegs

The thorax has six **true legs**—*three on each side—with claws for gripping. These legs will become six long butterfly legs.*

A caterpillar digests its food inside its abdomen. On the outside, the abdomen has ten **prolegs**. *These little stumps have hooks for clinging to plants.*

Too big for its skin

The caterpillar eats a lot and grows quickly, but its skin does not grow along with its body. The skin gets so tight that the caterpillar has to **molt**, or shed its skin. The caterpillar does not shed its coat only once! It sheds four times while it is still growing. After each molt, the caterpillar pulls itself out of its old skin. It then rubs off its **face mask**, which is the black skin on its face.

A new face mask grows over the caterpillar's bigger head.

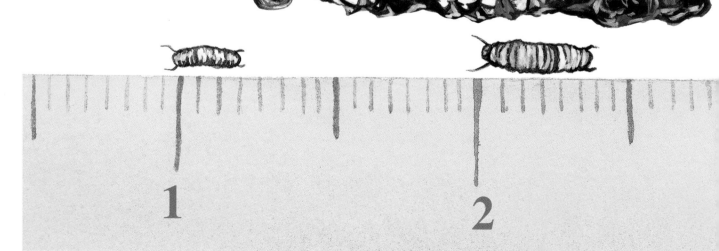

1   2

Growing and molting

A soft new skin forms under the tight old skin that the caterpillar sheds. After the caterpillar molts, the new skin hardens around its bigger body. The caterpillar grows and molts again. It is twice as big as it was the first time it shed its skin! It doubles its size again by the third molt. It is now almost one inch (2.5 cm) long.

Almost there

By the fourth molt, the caterpillar has grown even more! It is now almost fully grown. The growing stage between each molt is called an **instar**.

The caterpillar eats each coat it sheds. The coat is full of nutrients.

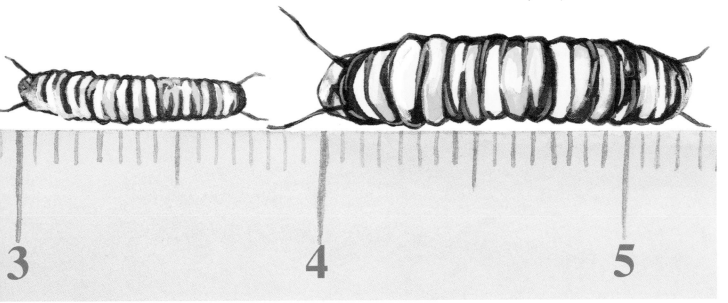

Taking a walk

After the caterpillar molts the fourth time, it takes a long walk. It looks for the perfect place to get ready for the next stage of its life cycle. The caterpillar shoots a silk string from its spinneret. The silk is like a rope ladder. The caterpillar uses the silk to pull itself over leaves, rocks, and branches.

The right spot

The caterpillar keeps moving until it finds a safe place from which to hang, such as a leaf or twig. When it finds a suitable spot, it starts to squirt silk.

The caterpillar turns its head from side to side, over and over, to make a silk mat. Then it makes a tiny silk knob, called a **button,** on the mat. The caterpillar will attach itself to this button just before it begins the next stage of its life cycle.

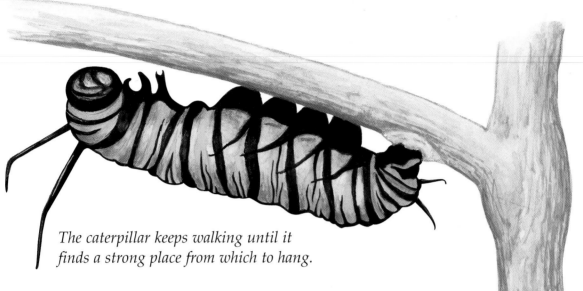

The caterpillar keeps walking until it finds a strong place from which to hang.

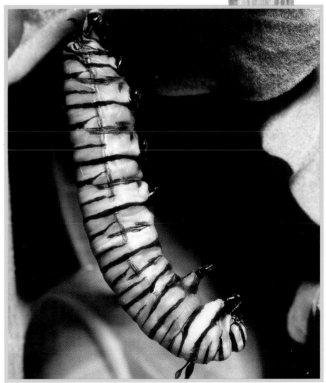

The caterpillar uses the hooks on its last set of prolegs to attach itself to the button on its silk mat.

The caterpillar then uncurls itself until it is hanging upside down.

17

Amazing change!

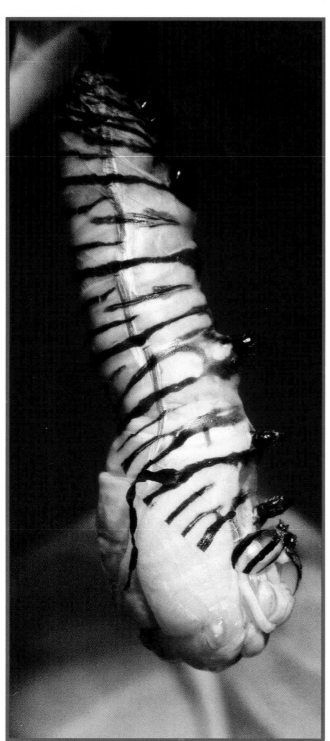

While the caterpillar hangs upside down, it molts for the last time. Its skin splits from head to tail. The caterpillar wriggles free of its skin without letting go of the button. Goodbye, stripes!

Hello, pupa!

Once the caterpillar is free of its old skin, a hard case forms around its body. The case is called a chrysalis. The insect inside the chrysalis is now called a pupa.

Caterpillar soup

The caterpillar's body changes completely inside the chrysalis. It **dissolves**, or breaks down, into a green liquid. Butterfly parts such as wings start forming in this soupy mixture.

Inside the chrysalis

The chrysalis protects the changing pupa. At first, the chrysalis looks green because the caterpillar is dissolved inside. By the second week, the chrysalis is clearer. Look carefully! You can see the pupa starting to change into a butterfly. When the chrysalis becomes totally clear, the butterfly is ready to **emerge**, or come out of its case.

Third stage

The pupa is the third stage in the life cycle of all butterflies. Each type of butterfly pupa has a different chrysalis. An owl butterfly, for example, emerges from a chrysalis that looks like a dead leaf. Find the owl butterfly on page 5.

A completely new look

It takes some time—and two or three pushes—for the butterfly to break out of the chrysalis.

The newly formed butterfly pushes itself out of the chrysalis. Its wings are wet and weak, and its body is full of liquid. The monarch hangs from the empty chrysalis and flaps its wings. It pumps liquid from its body into the black veins of its wings. The wings grow bigger and stronger as the veins fill with liquid.

Taste bad, stay safe

The butterfly cannot move while its wings are drying, but the milkweed leaves it ate as a caterpillar keep it safe. The leaves contained a poison that is now in the butterfly's wings. The poison can make birds and other animals sick. Hungry birds soon find out that even though orange wings look great, they taste terrible. They learn to stay clear of monarchs!

Metamorphosis

The change from caterpillar to butterfly is a **metamorphosis**. The word "metamorphosis" means "change of **form**," or shape. Metamorphosis is the total change of an animal's body from one form to another. After metamorphosis, there is no longer a caterpillar. Instead, there is a beautiful butterfly.

A brand new life

With its new body, a butterfly leads a new life. As a caterpillar, it could not go far on its stubby legs. As a butterfly, it can fly long distances. The caterpillar did not see well, but the butterfly has good vision. The caterpillar chewed leaves using its strong jaws. The butterfly drinks nectar through its proboscis.

The butterfly flaps its wings until they are fully spread and waits for them to dry so it can fly away.

21

Male and female

scent scales

Both monarchs on this page are male. They have black scent scales on their hind wings.

Can you spot the difference between the butterflies on this page and those on the next page? Male monarchs have a dark dot on each of their hind wings. The dots are made up of **scent scales**. When a male is ready to **mate**, or make babies, it rubs its scent scales with its hind legs. Rubbing its scales creates a scent that attracts females.

One-time parents

A monarch mates only once in its lifetime. A male and female mate so the female can lay eggs. The butterflies do not live long after they mate. The eggs hatch quickly, however, and the life cycle starts all over again.

These monarchs are females.
They do not have scent scales.

Flying south

Monarchs are the only butterflies that **migrate**, or travel long distances. Cold weather kills monarchs, so those born in autumn must migrate to warm places for the winter. Most North American monarchs fly to Mexico or California. Since they must travel so far, they often **glide**, or let the wind carry them. The monarchs travel south in huge flocks. Millions of monarchs fill the skies! When they reach their winter home, they rest in tall trees. So many monarchs pile on top of one another that they totally cover the trees! They stay very still to save energy.

Not all monarchs migrate. Most go through their life cycle in one place. Monarchs born in the early fall, however, must journey to a warmer climate to avoid harsh winter weather.

24

Heading home

In April or May, the monarchs start to fly north. On this journey, the monarchs fly in smaller groups than before. They are heading home, but they will not make it all the way. They stop in areas with milkweed plants to mate and lay eggs. The butterflies die after mating, but their eggs hatch, and the life cycle starts again.

Starting over

The new caterpillars become pupas, change into monarch butterflies, and continue the northbound trip their parents started. They, too, stop to mate and lay eggs, starting the life cycle yet again. Before the butterflies reach home, the life cycle will have been completed up to six times!

25

Monarchs in danger

Monarchs lay eggs only on milkweed. If they cannot find healthy milkweed plants, monarchs will not lay eggs. People build roads and buildings on fields where milkweed grows, and they kill milkweed because they think it is ugly. You can help monarchs by convincing your parents and neighbors not to kill these plants. Get a group of your friends to help you plant milkweed or move it from gardens to wild areas.

This milkweed was sprayed with chemicals. Monarchs will not lay eggs here anymore. If they do not find other milkweed plants, their life cycle cannot continue.

Fewer places to rest

Year after year, monarchs fly to Mexico and California for the winter. They return to the same places and often to the same trees! These winter sites have just the right **climate** and plants and are the only areas where the monarchs can survive. Unfortunately, the sites are getting smaller. People are cutting down trees to sell the wood and clearing the land to make roads and buildings. There are laws to protect some of the monarch winter sites, but other sites are still in danger of disappearing.

27

Welcome, butterflies!

Butterflies do an important job. They spread **pollen**. As butterflies drink nectar from flowers, pollen from the flowers sticks to their bodies. This pollen rubs off on the other flowers that the butterflies visit. To make new plants, pollen must be spread from one plant to another.

Many butterflies die because the flowers on which they feed are sprayed with **pesticides**. These chemicals are meant to kill pests, but they kill helpful insects, too. A garden without chemicals is healthier for all living things. For a butterfly-friendly garden, ask your family not to use pesticides.

Butterfly gardens

Like monarchs, many other butterflies are losing the plants they need to survive. You can help butterflies in your area by planting the flowers on which they like to feed and lay eggs. Favorite nectar plants include zinnia, black-eyed Susan, marigold, sweet William, verbena, and lantana. Butterflies lay eggs on daisies, snapdragons, hollyhocks, clover, violets, and dill plants.

Pesticides and other gardening chemicals harm butterflies. They also hurt animals, such as birds, which eat butterflies and moths.

Rest for a minute

Make sure your garden is in a sunny spot and is sheltered from the wind. Butterflies love to stop and rest in the sun! If you set out a shallow pan of water, you might see a butterfly stop for a drink.

Butterfly houses offer shelter from harsh weather and predators. Butterflies slip in through the slots, where enemies cannot follow.

Raise a monarch

If you want to watch a butterfly go through its life cycle, you can raise a monarch butterfly yourself. You must promise that you will allow the butterfly to fly away as soon as it is ready! Make sure you have enough time to care for a caterpillar before you decide to raise one, and ask your parents for permission before you start.

You will need:

- a large clean jar
- a metal lid or a cloth with holes to cover the jar
- milkweed leaves
- a sturdy twig
- an adult to help you with some of the steps
- a notebook in which to record your observations

1. Cover the bottom of a large jar with gravel or leaves. Ask an adult to help you poke holes in the lid. If your jar does not have a lid, use a cloth with small holes such as cheesecloth. You can also use part of a nylon stocking.

2. Find a milkweed leaf with eggs or a caterpillar on it. Break off the leaf, put it into the jar, and cover the jar with the lid or cloth. Do not touch the caterpillar or the eggs! Make sure the caterpillar has light, but do not place it in direct sunlight.

3. Each day, add fresh milkweed leaves and take away the old leaves. The caterpillar will need 20 to 30 leaves over the next few days. Make sure you also have a twig in the jar. Why will it need a twig?

4. Check on the caterpillar often. Keep track of its molts and any other changes. After the last molt, the caterpillar will hang from the twig you put into the jar and become a pupa.

5. The pupa will change each day until it breaks out of its chrysalis as a butterfly. When its wings are dry, the butterfly will start to flap them. It is getting ready to fly away. Goodbye, butterfly!

Watching butterflies is fun, but remember that touching a butterfly can damage its wings!

Glossary

climate The long-term weather conditions in an area, including temperature, rainfall, and wind

habitat The natural place where a plant or animal is found

larva A baby insect after it hatches from an egg

lens The part of the eye that bends light to create images

nectar A sweet liquid in flowers

organ A part of the body that does an important job, such as the heart

pollen A powder in flowers that is needed to make new flowers

roost To rest or sleep on a perch

scales Tiny structures that cover a butterfly's wings

tentacles An insect's feelers

yolk The part of an egg that feeds the growing baby inside

Index

1 2 3 4 5 6 7 8 9 0 Printed in the U.S.A. 1 0 9 8 7 6 5 4 3 2